Saving Energy

Jacqueline Dineen

Watts Books
London • New York • Sydney

Watts Books
96 Leonard Street
London EC2A 4RH

Franklin Watts Australia
14 Mars Road
Lane Cove
NSW 2060

UK ISBN: 0 7496 1449 8

10 9 8 7 6 5 4 3 2 1

Editor: Claire Llewellyn
Design: Caroline Ginesi
Artwork: Michael Lye
Cover artwork: Hugh Dixon
Picture research: Alison Renwick

A CIP catalogue record for this book is available from the British Library

Dewey Decimal Classification 333.791

Printed in Italy by G. Canale & SpA

Contents

Why save energy?

A car will not run without **fuel** such as petrol or diesel. Fuel gives it **energy**. We use a great deal of energy every day. We use it to heat and light our homes and to work machinery. Planes, trains and cars use huge amounts of energy. All this energy is supplied by burning fuels. The big problem is that our supplies of fuel are running out.

▽ Aircraft need powerful engines to lift them off the ground. These engines burn enormous amounts of fuel.

Using up the fuel

Most of the energy we use comes from coal, oil and gas. These are all **fossil fuels**, which took millions of years to form and cannot be replaced quickly. Power stations burn fossil fuels to make electricity. Before the days of electricity, people were using fuels quite slowly. Now we are using them so fast that they could run out within 100 years.

▷ Today we have machines to do most jobs. Housework can be done quickly, but the machines run on electricity.

▽ 100 years ago people washed their clothes by hand. It was hard work.

ARIEL
Hotpoint

Life without fossil fuels

Imagine what life would be like without fossil fuels. We would not have electricity at the flick of a switch. There would be no lights and it would be difficult to keep warm. We would have to burn wood for fires and for cooking. Machines in homes, offices and factories could not operate. There would be no petrol – and no vehicles.

▽ This shopping centre would grind to a halt without electricity.

▷ People couldn't get to work without fuel. Trains run on diesel oil or electricity from overhead cables.

▽ Without oil, there would be no petrol to drive machines like these. Farmers would have to harvest their crops by hand again.

What can we do?

We have to use fossil fuels more carefully. One way to do this is to use less energy. Many people waste electricity, for example. They forget about saving energy, but there are many easy ways of doing this. Another way to save fossil fuels is to find new ways to produce the energy we need.

▽ Our coal reserves are running out and mines are being closed. This mine was shut down in 1967 after a fire destroyed the main coal seam.

▷ Oil is used to make plastic bags and containers, but most of these will end up in the bin.

▽ The solar panels on this roof use the sun's energy to heat the water in the house. This saves electricity – and fossil fuels.

New ideas

Many power stations produce electricity by burning huge amounts of coal, oil or gas. The burning fuel boils water to make steam for driving the **generator**. Power stations are looking at ways of saving fuel. Some burn rubbish instead of fuel. Electricity can also be produced using the natural energy of the sun, wind and flowing water.

▷ Electricity can be produced by using the wind to drive machinery.

▽ Many power stations use coal. They need constant supplies to keep their boilers going.

Nuclear power

Nuclear power stations produce electricity in the same way as those using fossil fuels. The fuel they use is a **mineral** called uranium, which is found in some types of rock. Uranium can be made to produce great heat, and most of it can be **recycled**. But nuclear power can be dangerous and many people are worried about using it.

▷ Uranium is found in rocks near the Earth's surface as well as deep underground.

∇ Nuclear power stations have very high standards of safety. But what if something goes wrong?

▷ The mineral uranium has to be separated from the rock before it can be used as fuel.

Fears about nuclear power

The great danger with nuclear power is that uranium is **radioactive**. This means it gives off invisible rays which damage parts of our body and can kill.

The used-up fuel from a nuclear power station stays radioactive for thousands of years, and is very dangerous. Storing it safely is a very difficult problem.

▷ Nuclear energy can bring disaster. In 1986 a nuclear power station caught fire in Chernobyl in Russia. Ninety-two thousand people had to leave their homes. These flats are still deserted.

▽ Workers have to wear special clothing in some parts of a nuclear power station. This protects them from the radioactive fuel.

Saving fuel at home

Many people use more energy than they need to heat their homes because the buildings are not properly insulated. **Insulation** prevents heat from escaping through the roof and walls, and stops draughts around doors and windows.

Energy is also wasted when central heating boilers do not work **efficiently** and make a house uncomfortably hot.

▽ The people who live in this poorly-insulated house are wasting energy. Heat is escaping in many different ways.

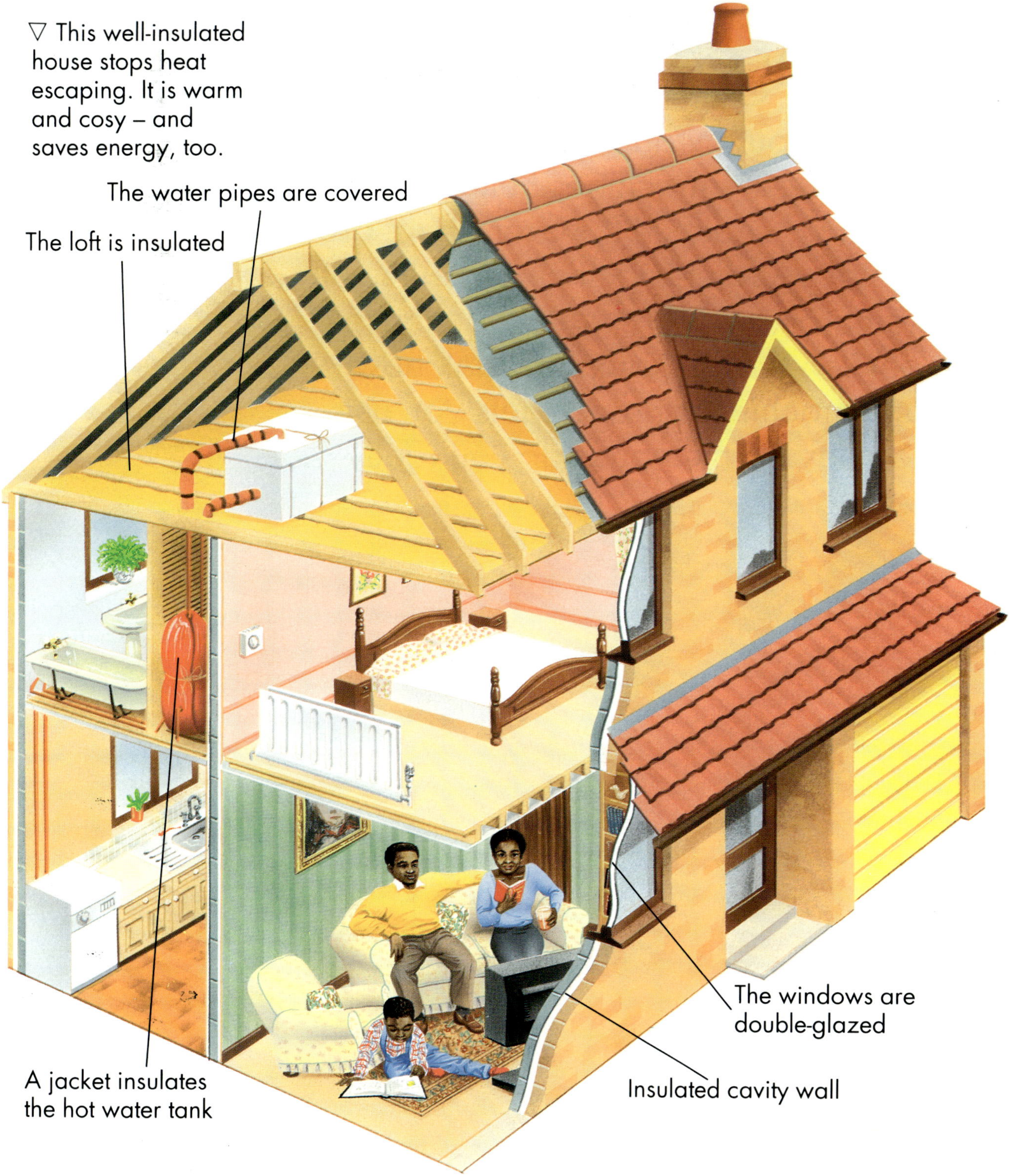

▽ This well-insulated house stops heat escaping. It is warm and cosy – and saves energy, too.

Saving electricity

No one would want to go back to the days before electric machines helped us with the household chores. However, there are many ways of using electricity more efficiently. Turning off the lights when you leave a room is a good example. Think how many machines and gadgets you use each day. Which ones do you really need?

▽ A busy kitchen uses a lot of electricity. There are all sorts of savings to be made.

▷ A shower is a good way to save energy. It uses less hot water than a bath.

▽ A tumble drier uses electricity to dry your clothes. Don't use it on a day when the sun and wind will do the job for free.

Saving on transport

▷ More and more motorists are leaving their car at home and finding other ways to get to work.

Cars and other vehicles run on petrol or diesel oil, which are both made from **crude oil**. Car makers are now designing smaller cars which use less fuel. Also, engines which run on diesel oil use less fuel than petrol engines. Some car makers have designed electric cars which run on batteries. They use far less energy than petrol-driven cars.

△ In the past, people liked big cars which used a lot of fuel.

▷ When oil became more expensive, they turned to smaller cars which were cheaper to run.

▷ Some towns have proper cycle lanes which make cycling safer. More of these would encourage people to use bikes.

Savings in industry

Many **industries** are now looking for ways to save energy. An example of this is in big supermarkets, where there are refrigerated display cases. The fridges use a lot of energy to keep cold, and they make a lot of heat in the process. A machine can now recover this heat and use it elsewhere – for example, to heat the water in the staff canteen.

▷ Old steel-making furnaces took so long to heat up, that they were left burning night and day. New furnaces heat up quickly and save energy.

▽ The heat from the back of these cold display cases can be used to warm other parts of the building.

Recycling saves fuel

Making new products from **raw materials** often uses more energy than recycling old ones. For example, **aluminium** is made from an **ore** called bauxite. A great deal of electricity is used to crush and heat the bauxite, to change it into aluminium. Recycling old aluminium cans uses less energy and is much more efficient.

▽ Mining bauxite to make aluminium. It takes 20 times more energy to make aluminium from bauxite than it does to recycle it.

▽ Old aluminium cans can be used to make new ones. Always take old cans to your local can bank.

▷ Squashing the old cans into bales makes them easier to handle. The bales are cleaned, melted and reshaped at a factory.

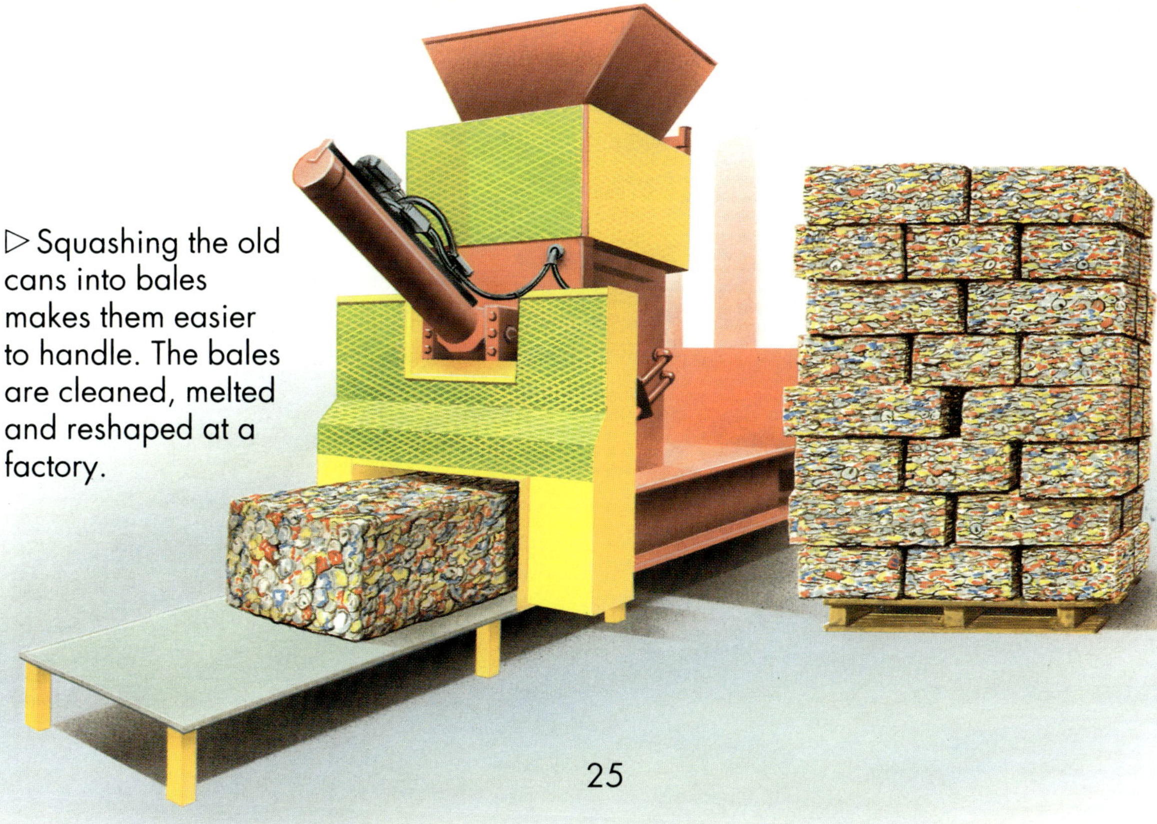

Recyclable materials

Steel is a light, strong metal which is widely used in building. It is made by melting iron, and mixing it with other materials. Like aluminium, however, it saves energy to recycle scrap steel rather than make it from new.

There are many other materials that can be recycled: glass, paper, used motor oil and some plastics. This all saves energy.

▽ Old glass bottles are collected in bottle banks. They are taken to a glassworks to be cleaned and melted.

▷ Old glass melts easily and can be reshaped into new bottles.

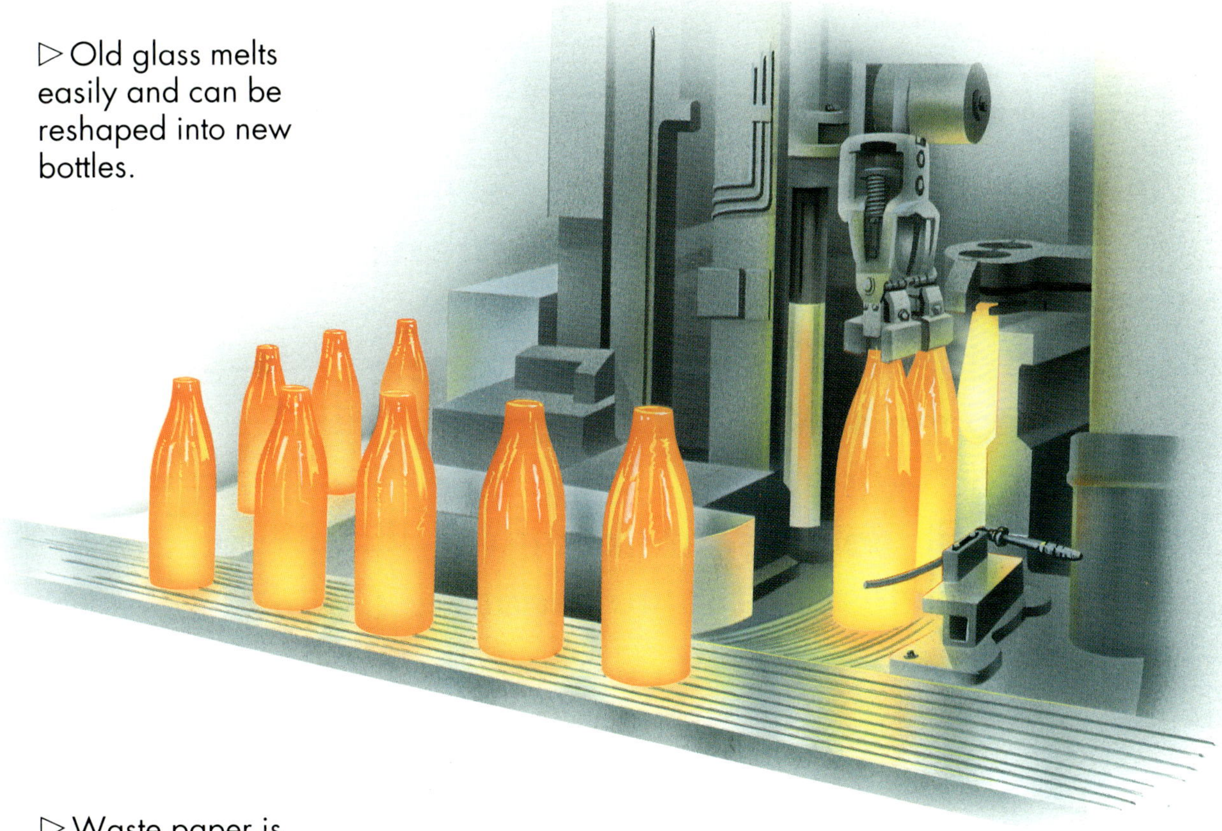

▷ Waste paper is baled up and recycled into many useful goods.

The greenhouse effect

Saving fossil fuels not only makes sense, but is good news for the **environment**. When we burn fossil fuels, we put carbon dioxide into the **atmosphere**. This can trap the sun's heat and make our planet too warm.

Burning fossil fuels also makes dirty fumes and pollutes the air we breathe.

▷ Petrol fumes pollute the air and make it difficult to breathe.

▽ Burning fossil fuels puts too much carbon dioxide in the air. It traps the sun's heat and makes our world too warm.

Things to do

- Think how you could cut down on the energy you use at home. Make a plan for your whole family to save energy.

- Design a poster to persuade people to recycle cans, bottles and newspapers.

- Draw a picture to illustrate life without fossil fuels.

Useful addresses:

Energy Efficiency Office
Department of the Environment
1 Palace Street
London SW1E 5HE

Understanding Electricity
The Electricity Association
30 Millbank
London SW1P 4RD

Glossary

aluminium A light metal.

atmosphere The layer of gases that surrounds the Earth.

crude oil The untreated oil which is pumped out of the ground.

efficient Working well without waste.

energy The power to do work and drive machines.

environment The natural world in which we live.

fossil fuel A fuel made from the remains of animals and plants which died millions of years ago. Oil, gas and coal are fossil fuels.

fuel A material, such as wood or petrol, which is burned to provide heat or energy.

generator A machine for producing electricity.

industry The work of factories or big organisations.

insulation A layer of material which prevents heat escaping.

mineral A natural substance which has not been formed from plants or animals. Rocks contain minerals.

ore Rock or soil which contains metal or other minerals which are mined.

pollute To spoil the air, land or water by making it dirty.

radioactive To give out harmful rays that carry energy.

raw material The natural substance from which something is made.

recycle To put something through a process where it is broken down so that it may be used again.

temperature How hot or cold a place is.

Index

Photographic credits:
J. Allan Cash 3, 8; Chris Faircough Colour Library 24, 26, 29; Robert Harding Picture Library 5, 6, 12, 21, 23; Peter Menzel/Science Photo Library 11.